coloring CReATIoNS 2

52 Creative Bible Lessons

Group

Loveland, Colorado

group.com

Group resources really work!

This Group resource incorporates our R.E.A.L. approach to ministry. It reinforces a growing friendship with Jesus, encourages long-term learning, and results in life transformation, because it's

Relational
Learner-to-learner interaction enhances learning and builds Christian friendships.

Experiential
What learners experience through discussion and action sticks with them up to 9 times longer than what they simply hear or read.

Applicable
The aim of Christian education is to equip learners to be both hearers and doers of God's Word.

Learner-based
Learners understand and retain more when the learning process takes into consideration how they learn best.

Coloring Creations 2
52 Creative Bible Lessons
Copyright © 2007 Group Publishing, Inc.

Visit our Web site: **group.com**

Credits
Chief Creative Officer: Joani Schultz
Author: Jody Brolsma
Editor: Jan Kershner
Senior Developer: Patty Anderson
Children's Ministry Champion: Christine Yount Jones
Copy Editor: Christy Fagerlin
Art Director: Andrea Filer
Cover Designer: RoseAnne Sather
Print Production Artist: Greg Longbons
Production Manager: DeAnne Lear

Unless otherwise indicated, all Scripture quotations are taken from the *Holy Bible,* New Living Translation, copyright © 1996, 2004. Used by permission of Tyndale House Publishers, Inc., Carol Stream, Illinois 60188. All rights reserved.

Library of Congress Cataloging-in-Publication Data

Coloring creations 2 : 52 new bible activity pages / [editor, Jan Kershner].
    p. cm.
Includes indexes.
ISBN 978-0-7644-3506-5 (pbk. : alk. paper) 1. Bible crafts. 2. Church work with children. 3. Christian education--Activity programs.
I. Kershner, Jan. II. Title. III. Title: Coloring creations two.
BS613.B67 2007
268'.432--dc22
                 2007011211

ISBN 978-0-7644-3506-5

10 9 8 7 6   16 15 14 13 12

Printed in the United States of America.

Contents

Introduction

You asked for it! And we listened!

We kept hearing, "When are you going to come out with another *Coloring Creations* book? My kids love it!" So here it is: *Coloring Creations 2: 52 New Bible Activity Pages.*

Like its predecessor, *Coloring Creations 2* looks like a coloring book, but it's much more! It's an *activity* page book. Each reproducible coloring page is based on a Bible story and Scripture verse, includes an activity to make the page 3-D, and even has an age-appropriate discussion guide to help you make the activity life-applicable. Each activity in this book is a chance for you to expand on a lesson, dig a little deeper into the Bible, and teach a valuable lesson to your students.

Perfect for those days when a lesson runs short or a sermon runs long, *Coloring Creations 2* offers new, creative...*and fast*...ideas for your classroom. And let's face it: kids love to color! Why not use their natural preference to help kids grow closer to Jesus?

Each activity is based on a Bible story, which makes this book a wonderful tool for any children's ministry leader. Simply locate the activity page in this book that best accompanies the story you're teaching and you've got an instant enhancement for your lesson. Plus, kids will have a fun craft activity to take home.

Each page also emphasizes a Scripture verse, which leads to a discussion section focused on life-application; the verses offer children a way to live out the lesson of the Bible story. If children are discovering the story of Creation, they'll learn to care for the wonderful world God created. If they hear the story of Zacchaeus, they'll understand that knowing Jesus can change their lives.

The pages in this book are *reproducible*, so the book belongs on your bookshelf where it can be pulled out and used again and again—for years.

Each coloring page is more than a coloring page: it's a 3-D, multi-sensory, super-tactile *creation!* Your kids will color the page...decorate it, cut it, fold it, paint it, and all around change it.

Each page is accompanied by instructions to help you turn pictures into 3-D masterpieces that help kids learn and remember the Bible story and the Scripture verse. The instructions are simple, the supplies general, and the process rewarding.

Coloring Creations 2 can help you transform coloring time into teaching time. With this book, coloring becomes more than busywork—it's a chance to engage your children in dialogue, to grow deeper relationships, and to teach lasting Bible truths!

Just use the indexes to locate the activity page that best fits your lesson, make a copy of the page for each child, gather the necessary supplies...and get started on an activity that will help your children grow closer to God!

Coloring Creations Kit

Many of the coloring pages in this book use basic supplies to transform the pages into craft projects kids love. Take a few moments to gather the following supplies and place them in a plastic box to use with this book. That way you'll always have the right supplies available at a moment's notice.

Tuck these items in your "Coloring Creations Kit":

- craft glue
- crayons
- colored pencils
- scissors
- glue sticks
- markers
- transparent tape
- safety scissors

When you see "Coloring Creations Kit" in a supply list, you'll know the basic supplies are already gathered and ready to use!

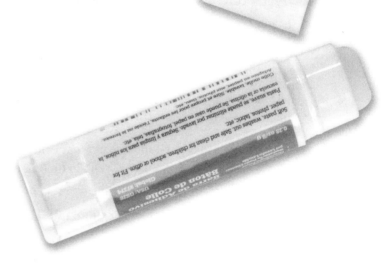

ALLERGY ALERT

Some of the projects in this book involve food. Be aware that some children have food allergies that can be dangerous. Know your children, and consult with parents about allergies their children may have. Also be sure to carefully read food labels, as hidden ingredients can cause allergy-related problems.

Choking Hazards!

Be aware that small objects can be choking hazards for younger children. Supervise children as they work with small objects such as dry cereal and wiggly eyes. If you have several young children in your class, you may want to substitute a larger object for the craft.

God Creates Our World

Genesis 1:1-25

What you need:

For each child...

• 1 copy of page 7

You'll also need...

• glitter glue
• cotton swabs
• paper plates
• cups of water
• watercolor paints
• Coloring Creations Kit

What to do:

Write children's names on their pages. Squeeze glitter glue onto paper plates, and set out the plates along with black crayons, cups of water, and watercolor paints.

1. Give each child an activity page. Point to the spaces between the earth, planets, and stars. Explain that before God made our world, everything was dark and black. Let children color between the earth, planets, and stars with a black crayon. (It's OK if they color over some of the stars.)

2. Tell children that God put lights in the sky. Let children use cotton swabs to dab glitter glue on the stars and planets.

3. Say the Scripture verse, and explain that God made the earth with his own hands, creating a special place for people to live. Let children dip their fingers in the water, and then into the watercolor paints to color the earth.

4. Tell children that God rested when he'd finished making the earth. Set the pictures aside to "rest" and dry.

Talk about:

Ask: • Why do you think God made the earth for us?
• How can you use your hands to thank God for all he made?

Say: The earth, stars, and planets all belong to God because he made them. We can thank God by using our hands to care for the things he's made. You can water flowers, feed your dog, or pick up trash to keep God's special world clean and beautiful! Let's use our hands right now to clap for God. *Lead children in applauding for God.*

Pray: Dear God, thank you for making the world with your very own hands. It's such a beautiful place! Help us use *our* hands to take good care of your world. In Jesus' name, amen.

"The earth is the Lord's, and everything in it"

(Psalm 24:1a).

Permission to photocopy this coloring page from *Coloring Creations 2: 52 New Bible Activity Pages* granted for local church use. Copyright © Group Publishing, Inc., 1515 Cascade Ave., Loveland, CO 80538. group.com

God Made Us Special

Genesis 1:26-27

What you need:

For each child...

• 1 copy of page 9

You'll also need...

• colored construction paper
• markers
• Coloring Creations Kit

What to do:

Write children's names on their pages. Cut out 2x3-inch rectangles from the construction paper, then cut out a smaller rectangle in the middle to create a "picture frame." You'll need one per child. Set out markers and glue.

1. Give each child an activity page. Ask children to tell you what they see on the paper, but to say, "God made…" before naming the item. For example, a child might say, "God made bears."

2. Let children use markers to color the picture. As children color, talk about other things God made. Say the Scripture verse, and ask children to think of something good about each item they're coloring.

3. When children have finished, explain that the most special thing God made was people, and that God loves the people he made.

4. Talk about how we keep pictures of people we love, and sometimes put the pictures in a frame. Give each child a construction paper frame, and let them glue the frame over the picture of Adam and Eve.

Talk about:

Ask: • Who are some special people God made?
• What makes those people so special?

Say: All of the things God made are good. But God made people extra special. God wants us to treat other people as his special creations. That means we say kind words, obey, and love others the way God does.

Pray: Dear God, thank you for making so many wonderful things. We're glad you made people to be so special. Help us treat others as your special creation. In Jesus' name, amen.

"Then God looked over all he had made, and he saw that it was very good!"

(Genesis 1:31a).

noah Builds the Ark

Genesis 6:5-17

What you need:

For each child...

• 1 copy of page 11

You'll also need...

• wood-grain self-adhesive shelf paper
• cups of water
• Coloring Creations Kit

What to do:

Write children's names on their pages. Cut the self-adhesive shelf paper into 1/2x2-inch strips, and peel back the backing halfway. Stick the strips to a table or counter where children can reach them.

1. Give each child an activity page, and direct them to color *only* Noah. Talk about how Noah loved and obeyed God. In fact, Noah was the only one in the whole world who loved and obeyed God!

2. Tell children that God wanted Noah to build a big boat called an ark, where Noah's family would be safe. Say that Noah obeyed God because he loved God. Read the Scripture verse, and have children repeat it with you. Explain that when we love God, we want to obey him. Point out that Noah's boat isn't quite finished and they'll need to work carefully to help him finish it.

3. Let children peel the backing from the strips and place them over the pieces of wood in the picture. When children have covered the entire boat with "wood," allow them to dip their fingers in the cups and drip water onto the "wood." Point out that the water doesn't soak into the wood, so everyone inside the boat will be safe.

Talk about:

Ask: • **What was hard about making your boat today?**
 • **Noah obeyed God when God told him to make the boat, even though it might have been hard. When is it hard for you to obey God?**

Say: **It wasn't easy for Noah to build the boat. He had to work hard! But he loved God and wanted to please God, so Noah obeyed.** Help each child wrap a strip of the sticky plastic around one of their fingers, as a reminder to "stick to it" when it's hard to obey God.

Pray: **God, we love you, and we want to obey you. You know that sometimes it's hard for us to obey. Give us the strength to stick to it, even when we may not want to do things your way. In Jesus' name, amen.**

"If you love me, obey my commandments"

(John 14:15).

Permission to photocopy this coloring page from *Coloring Creations 2: 52 New Bible Activity Pages* granted for local church use. Copyright © Group Publishing, Inc., 1515 Cascade Ave., Loveland, CO 80538. group.com

Safe in the Ark

Genesis 7:17-24

What you need:

For each child...
- 1 copy of page 13
- 1 16-ounce cup

You'll also need...
- spray bottles filled with water
- blue tempera paint
- tablespoon
- newspapers
- Coloring Creations Kit

What to do:

Write children's names on their pages. Add one tablespoon of blue tempera paint to the spray bottles. Set the nozzle to "mist." Set out crayons and cups. You may want to cover tables with newspaper.

1. Give each child an activity page, and point to the ark. Tell children that Noah was the only person in the whole world who loved and obeyed God, so God told Noah to build a big boat called an ark.

2. Let children use crayons to color the ark, the clouds, and the lightning.

3. Explain that after Noah and his family and lots and lots of animals were safe inside the ark, God made it rain for 40 days and nights. Say the Scripture verse, and tell children that God was watching over Noah and keeping him safe.

4. Give each child a 16-ounce cup, and have children turn the cup upside down over the ark. Then let children take turns spraying their papers with the "stormy" blue water. When children remove the cups, they'll see that the ark was "protected" from the "storm."

Talk about:

Ask:
- What do you think it was like for Noah inside the ark during the storm?
- When is a time God watched over you or your family?

Say: God takes care of us during real storms or when things in life are hard. That doesn't mean bad things won't happen. But you and I can trust that God is always watching over us.

Pray: God, it's good to know that you're watching over us all the time. Help us remember that we can always talk to you and trust you when we're afraid. In Jesus' name, amen.

"The Lord himself watches over you!"

(Psalm 121:5a).

The Rainbow Promise

Genesis 9:8-17

What you need:

For each child...

- 1 copy of page 15
- 1 coffee filter

You'll also need...

- watercolor paints
- cups of water
- paintbrushes
- Coloring Creations Kit

What to do:

Write children's names on their pages. Set out the supplies.

1. Give each child a coffee filter, and have children turn the filters upside down.

2. Demonstrate how to wet a paintbrush with plenty of paint and water, and drip the color on the over-turned coffee filter. As children drip colored "rain" on their filters, talk about how God sent lots of rain upon the earth. In fact, the earth was completely flooded with water! Remind children that God kept Noah, his family, and lots of animals safe on a big boat called an ark.

3. When children have covered their coffee filters with color, set the filters aside to dry. (The coffee filters will dry quickly if they're set in a sunny place.) If necessary for ownership purposes, write each child's name on a sheet of paper and place his or her filter on the paper to dry.

4. Give each child an activity page, and let kids color the picture of Noah and the ark. Talk about how the flood waters dried up—just like the coffee filters are drying right now. Soon, everyone could leave the ark.

5. Explain that God sent a colorful rainbow as a reminder of his promise to never flood the whole earth again. Read the Scripture verse, and have children repeat it with you. Say that every time they see a rainbow, they can remember the verse. Help each child scrunch and shape his or her filter into an arch shape and tape it to the rainbow on the picture.

Talk about:

Ask: • If you had been Noah, what's the first thing you would have done when you got out of the ark?

• How can you thank God today for promising to take care of us?

Say: God put the rainbow in the sky so that every time people see it, they could remember how much God loves us. God keeps his promises to us, just as he kept his promise to Noah.

Pray: God, thank you for loving us and keeping your promises to us. We praise you for being so faithful and loving to us. In Jesus' name, amen.

"The Lord always keeps his promises"

(Psalm 145:13b).

Permission to photocopy this coloring page from *Coloring Creations 2: 52 New Bible Activity Pages* granted for local church use. Copyright ©
Group Publishing, Inc., 1515 Cascade Ave., Loveland, CO 80538. group.com

God Promises Abraham Countless Descendants

Genesis 15:5; 17:1-7

What you need:

For each child...

• 1 copy of page 17

You'll also need...

• shakers of glitter
• Coloring Creations Kit

What to do:

Write children's names on their pages. Set out glue, crayons, and shakers of glitter.

1. Give each child an activity page. As children color the picture, explain that the man—named Abraham—was very old. Even though Abraham didn't have any children, God promised that Abraham would have lots and lots and lots of grandchildren. In fact, God said Abraham would have more descendents—that means grandchildren and great-grandchildren and great-great-grandchildren—than there are stars!

2. Help children dot glue on each of the stars, counting each one as they add glue.

3. Have each child sprinkle some glitter into his or her hand and try to count the pieces. Say that just as we can't count the grains of glitter, God told Abraham that he would have more descendents than he could count. Talk about how that probably seemed impossible—like it couldn't happen—since Abraham was old and didn't even have *one* child.

4. Let children sprinkle glitter on the glue to make the stars twinkle. As they add glitter, explain that God kept his promise. Lead children in saying the Scripture verse as a reminder that God can do anything.

Talk about:

Ask: • **What do you think Abraham thought when he heard God's promise?**

• **Is there anything *you* think is too hard for God? Tell me about it.**

Say: **Abraham might have wondered if God could really make him have more descendents than there were stars. But nothing is impossible with God. God did amazing things in Abraham's life, and he has plans to do amazing things in *your* life, too!**

Pray: **God, we love you and we're so glad that nothing is impossible with you. Thank you for having great plans for our lives—even if we can't imagine what they'll be. Help us to trust you and wait excitedly to see the incredible things you can do. In Jesus' name, amen.**

"For nothing is impossible with God"

(Luke 1:37).

Abraham Obeys and God Saves Isaac

Genesis 22:1-18

What you need:

For each child...
• 1 copy of page 19

You'll also need...
• gray construction paper
• brown chenille wires
• Coloring Creations Kit

What to do:

Write children's names on their pages. Cut 1-inch "rocks" from gray construction paper (you'll need about 10 per child). Cut brown chenille wires into 2-inch "sticks." Write each child's name on his or her page. Set out the chenille wire segments, glue, crayons, and paper circles.

1. Give each child an activity page, and point out Abraham and his son, Isaac. Tell children that God told Abraham to give up his son, Isaac. Let children color the grass as you tell how Abraham and Isaac walked to a special place to obey God.

2. Explain that God told Abraham to build an altar—a pile of stones. As children glue paper "stones" to their activity pages, remind children that Abraham loved Isaac but he still obeyed God.

3. Tell children that God told Abraham to pick up sticks to make a fire on the altar. Let children glue chenille wire to the sticks in Abraham and Isaac's arms. Point out that Abraham obeyed God and gathered sticks to make the fire.

4. Say that when it was time to give up his son, God sent a ram (or sheep) for Abraham to sacrifice instead. He didn't have to give up his son after all! Abraham was glad he'd trusted God. Read the Scripture verse, and have children repeat it. Remind them that they can always trust God, just as Abraham did.

Talk about:

Ask: • **God told Abraham to give up his precious son. Do you think it was easy for Abraham to obey God? Why or why not?**

• **Abraham trusted God, even though it was hard. When was a time you or your family trusted God?**

Say: **God told Abraham to do something really hard. Abraham obeyed because he trusted God. That made God happy. You and I can obey God, too. Even if we have to do something hard, we can trust and obey God.**

Pray: **Dear God, sometimes it's hard to trust and obey you. Help us to be brave and do what you want us to do...even when it's hard. We love you and trust you. In Jesus' name, amen.**

"Trust in the Lord with all your heart"

(Proverbs 3:5a).

Joseph in the Well

Genesis 37:18-30

What you need:

For each child...
- 1 copy of page 21
- 1 craft stick

You'll also need...
- colorful fabric, cut into 3-inch squares (approximately)
- Coloring Creations Kit

What to do:

Write children's names on their pages. On each paper, cut a curved slit just above the top row of stones in the well to make an opening in the center of the well. Carefully cut out Joseph's face. Set out markers, glue, transparent tape, pieces of fabric, and craft sticks.

1. Give each child a craft stick, and have children glue Joseph's face to one end. Explain that Joseph was a boy who had lots of brothers.

2. Let children tape a piece of fabric to the craft stick while you explain that Joseph's father had given him a beautiful, colorful coat. Tell children that Joseph's brothers were jealous because of the coat. Distribute activity pages and have children color the jealous, mad brother.

3. Say that Joseph's brothers got so mad that they did something mean. They took off Joseph's beautiful coat (have children take the fabric "coat" off of the stick figure and tape it near the well on the picture). Say that the brothers then put Joseph into a dirty well. Let children slip their stick figure into the slit in the well.

4. Read the Scripture verse to the children, and talk about how sad Joseph must have felt when he was in the well. Encourage children to use their stick figures to retell the story to each other.

Talk about:

Ask: • How do you think Joseph felt when his brothers were mean to him?

• When has someone been unkind to you?

• How can your family members show kindness to each other?

Say: God wants us to be kind to each other. Even though Joseph's brothers were mad and jealous, they still should have been nice to Joseph. When we're feeling bad or angry, God still wants us to be kind and loving to our friends and family members.

Pray: Dear God, it's hard to be nice when we feel bad or mad. Give us the strength to be kind to our friends and family members, no matter how we feel. Show us new ways to be kind. In Jesus' name, amen.

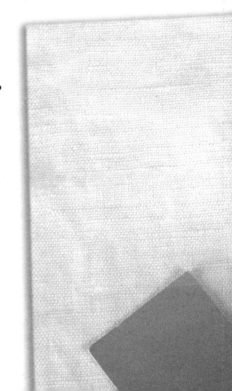

"Be kind to each other"

(Ephesians 4:32a).

Permission to photocopy this coloring page from *Coloring Creations 2: 52 New Bible Activity Pages* granted for local church use. Copyright © Group Publishing, Inc., 1515 Cascade Ave., Loveland, CO 80538. group.com

Joseph Does His Best

Genesis 39:1-6

What you need:

For each child...
- 1 copy of page 23
- 1 16-ounce cup

You'll also need...
- small treats such as bear-shaped cookies, small crackers, fruit, or candy
- Coloring Creations Kit

What to do:

Write children's names on their pages. Set out cups, treats, transparent tape, and markers.

1. Give each child an activity page. Instruct children to color the picture, being sure to do their very best coloring. While children color, point to the picture of Joseph and explain that Joseph worked for a rich man named Potiphar. Tell children that Joseph did his best when he served Potiphar.

2. Help children each wrap their pictures around a cup and tape it to the cup. Have kids form pairs, and direct them to fill their special cups with a tasty treat for their partners.

3. Read the Scripture verse aloud, and have kids repeat it a few times. Then have partners trade cups while saying the verse. While children enjoy the treats, talk about how nice it is when someone does their very best for us.

Talk about:

Ask:
- Joseph helped out in Potiphar's house. How can you help out in your house?
- Who is someone you'd like to do your very best for? Why?

Say: Joseph had to work hard—it wasn't always easy to do his best. When you and I have something hard to do, we can remember this verse. Let's ask God to help us do our best all the time.

Pray: God, sometimes it's hard to do our best. Please help us work cheerfully—just like we were working for you. We want to do our best for you. In Jesus' name, amen.

"And whatever you do or say, do it as a representative of the Lord Jesus"

(adapted from Colossians 3:23a).

Joseph Forgives His Brothers

Genesis 42:1–46:34

What you need:

For each child...
- 1 copy of page 25

You'll also need...
- Coloring Creations Kit

What to do:

Cut the pictures in half, separating Joseph and the brother he's hugging. Write children's names on both parts of one activity page. Attach small strips of transparent tape to the edge of a table so they're easy for children to use. Set out crayons.

1. Have children cover their eyes while you hide the pictures of Joseph (wearing the royal headgear) around the room.

2. Give children the part of their activity page that shows Joseph's brothers. Tell children that these men had been mean to their brother Joseph. But they were sorry for being mean, so they went to find Joseph. Help children find their pictures of Joseph.

3. When everyone has both halves of the picture, show children how to tape the two parts together. Say that even though the brothers had been mean, Joseph hugged his brothers and forgave them. Lead children in saying the Scripture verse as they hold up their taped pictures.

4. Let children color the pictures to show how happy everyone was to be together again.

Talk about:

Ask:
- How do you think Joseph felt when he saw his brothers for the first time in many years?
- When is a time you had to forgive someone?
- When is a time you did something wrong and someone had to forgive you?

Say: God forgives us when we're sorry for the wrong things we do. When people hurt our feelings or make us sad, God wants us to forgive them, too. Forgiveness brings families together again. Forgiveness lets friends have fun again! When someone has been mean, you can ask God to help you forgive just like Joseph forgave his brothers.

Pray: Dear God, we're so glad that *you* forgive *us*. We want to forgive others, too. Help us to be loving and help us to forgive, even when our feelings are hurt. In Jesus' name, amen.

"Remember, the Lord forgave you, so you must forgive others"

(Colossians 3:13b).

God Calls Moses to Be His Helper

Exodus 3:1-12

What you need:

For each child...

• 1 copy of page 27

You'll also need...

• paintbrushes
• water
• cups
• yellow and red tissue paper
• Coloring Creations Kit

What to do:

Write children's names on their pages. Squeeze glue into cups, and add a few teaspoons of water to thin the glue. Set out paintbrushes, crayons, and the tissue paper.

1. Hand each child an activity page and point to Moses. Explain that Moses was a man who loved God. As children color Moses, say that he was a shepherd who was out watching his sheep when something amazing happened to him.

2. Show children the bush, and explain that Moses saw a bush that was on fire...but it didn't burn up. Let children tear short strips of tissue paper and glue them to the bush. (The yellow and red will mix with the water in the glue to make a bright orange "flame.")

3. Tell children that God spoke to Moses through the fire. God asked Moses to be his special helper... someone who would do mighty things in God's name.

Talk about:

Ask: • Do you think Moses wanted to be God's special helper? Why or why not?

• How can you be God's special helper at home? At church?

Say: Moses was surprised when God called him to be a helper, but Moses loved God, and he obeyed. Read the Scripture verse aloud. We can obey God, just as Moses did. God has great plans for you to be a helper, too! God wants you to show his love and tell people about his Son, Jesus. You might be surprised at the ways you can be a helper for God!

Pray: God, we love you. We want to help others know and love you. Help us to obey you and to be your helpers. In Jesus' name, amen.

"I obey your commandments with all my heart"

(Psalm 119:69b).

Permission to photocopy this coloring page from *Coloring Creations 2: 52 New Bible Activity Pages* granted for local church use. Copyright © Group Publishing, Inc., 1515 Cascade Ave., Loveland, CO 80538. group.com

God Provides Manna and Quail

Exodus 16:1-35

What you need:

For each child...

• 1 copy of page 29

You'll also need...

• tan paper
• any kind of cereal with flakes
• Coloring Creations Kit

 ALLERGY ALERT

What to do:

Write children's names on their pages. Cut tan paper into small pieces. Set out glue and crayons.

1. Tell children that the Israelites, God's special people, were traveling to a special land God wanted to give them. But they were running out of food! Tell children that the people went to sleep hungry. Have children close their eyes and pretend to sleep.

2. Scatter the paper pieces on the floor, then let children open their eyes. Hand each child an activity page, and show them how the Israelites found food on the ground—a special food made by God! Repeat the Scripture verse, and talk about how happy the Israelites were when they found the food God sent.

3. Let children collect paper pieces and glue them to their pictures, filling the bowls the Israelites are holding. Explain that the Bible says that the food looked like flakes. Then let children color the pages. When everyone has finished coloring, give children flakes of cereal to taste.

Talk about:

Ask: • What did God provide (or give) to the Israelites?

• What things does God provide for you?

• How can you thank God for all he's given you?

Say: God's people had to trust that he would feed them. And they were sure happy when he did! We can trust God to give us what we need, too. God is amazing!

Pray: Amazing God, you are so awesome! Thank you for giving us what we need. We love you. In Jesus' name, amen.

"Oh, the joys of those who trust the Lord"

(Psalm 40:4a).

Ruth Goes With Naomi

Ruth 1:1-18

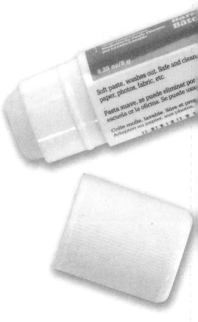

What you need:

For each child...

• 1 copy of page 31

ALLERGY ALERT

You'll also need...

• cinnamon
• sugar
• spoons
• cups
• sand
• Coloring Creations Kit

What to do:

Write children's names on their pages. Set out cinnamon, sugar, spoons, cups, markers, and glue or glue sticks.

1. Give children their activity pages, and show them the two women. Explain that Naomi was sad because her sons and husband had died. Let children taste the unsweetened cinnamon. Discuss how Naomi's life wasn't sweet.

2. Point to Ruth and tell children that Ruth was a friend to Naomi. Naomi wanted to move away by herself, but Ruth wanted to go with her. Let children taste the sugar and think about how sweet and kind Ruth was.

3. Have children spread glue on the ground where Ruth and Naomi are walking. Let children sprinkle sand on the glue to make a dusty road.

4. While children color the picture, read the Scripture verse and talk about ways we can be sweet friends to each other.

Talk about:

Ask: • When has someone in your family been sad like Naomi?

• How can you be a sweet friend like Ruth?

Say: Ruth was a sweet friend to Naomi. She stayed with her and helped her. Hey, that reminds me of God! He stays with us and helps us. God is our best friend!

Pray: Lord, thank you for being our best friend. Help us to be sweet friends to others. In Jesus' name, amen.

"Kind words are like honey—sweet to the soul and healthy for the body"

(Proverbs 16:24).

Ruth Gathers Grain

Ruth 1:19–2:3

What you need:

For each child…

• 1 copy of page 33

ALLERGY ALERT

You'll also need…

• brown or tan raffia ribbon
• a bowl
• Shredded Wheat cereal
• Coloring Creations Kit

What to do:

Write children's names on their pages. Cut the raffia into short pieces a few inches long, and place them in a bowl. Set out glue and crayons or markers.

1. Give each child an activity page. As children color the picture, explain that Ruth had to work hard to gather wheat to make bread for herself and Naomi.

2. Let children spread glue on the wheat in the picture. Direct kids to "gather" pieces of raffia and press the pieces on the glue. Talk about how Ruth had to pick up the small pieces of wheat that other people left behind.

3. Read the Scripture verse aloud, and talk about how Ruth never got tired of helping Naomi and doing good. When their pictures are finished, allow children to nibble Shredded Wheat cereal. Explain that the cereal is made of grain, just like the grain that Ruth gathered. Talk about how glad Ruth and Naomi were to have food to eat.

Talk about:

Ask: • How did Ruth help Naomi?

• What would have happened if Ruth had given up and stopped gathering the wheat?

• How can you help your family?

Say: Ruth helped Naomi by working hard to collect wheat. That was a hard job, and she probably got tired. Maybe she even wanted to quit! But she knew that she was doing a good thing that would help her family. Let's ask God to help us do good things for our families.

Pray: Loving God, thank you for giving us strong bodies and minds so we can do good things for our families. Please help us never get tired of doing good things like…(Go around the group, and let children fill in phrases of things that they can do to serve their families.) **In Jesus' name, amen.**

"So let's not get tired of doing what is good"

(Galatians 6:9a).

Friends Help Each Other

1 Samuel 20:1-40

What you need:

For each child...

- 1 copy of page 35
- a 2-inch circle cut from gray or brown construction paper

You'll also need...

- Coloring Creations Kit

What to do:

Write children's names on their pages. Cut a "rock" from gray or brown construction paper for each child. Set out glue and crayons or markers.

1. Give each child an activity page and a "rock." Let children color their pictures.

2. Tell children that David—the boy who is hiding—was best friends with Jonathan—the boy shooting the arrow. Jonathan's father wanted to hurt David, so David had to run away. Explain that Jonathan told David to hide while Jonathan found out if it was safe to come back. Talk about how Jonathan helped David be safe.

3. Have children glue the top part of the rock over David, so they can lift up the bottom of the rock to see him.

4. Tell children that Jonathan sent a secret message to David by shooting his arrow very far. Then David knew that it wasn't safe to come back.

Talk about:

Ask: • **How do you think David felt when he couldn't be with his best friend, Jonathan?**

Read the Scripture verse aloud.

• **Who is a good friend to you?**

• **What does that person do to help you?**

Say: **Good friends help each other. A friend helps you feel happy when you're sad. A friend helps you make good choices. A friend helps you know and follow Jesus. Let's thank God for our good friends!**

Pray: **God, thank you for being our friend. I'm thankful for my friends here today. (Say each child's name, and thank God for that child.) Show us how to help our friends love and follow you each day. In Jesus' name, amen.**

"A real friend sticks closer than a brother"

(Proverbs 18:24b).

Friends Help Each Other   35

Friends Keep Friends in Their Hearts

1 Samuel 20:41-42

What you need:

For each child...
- 1 copy of page 37
- 1 heart-shaped sticker

You'll also need...
- Coloring Creations Kit

What to do:

Write children's names on their pages. Set out stickers and markers.

1. Give each child an activity page, and allow kids to color their pictures.

2. Point out the sad man in the chair, and explain that this is Jonathan. Tell children that Jonathan was sad because he missed his best friend, David. Show children the picture of David running away. Talk about how Jonathan's father didn't like David and wanted to hurt him.

3. Show children how to fold the right side of the page inward so the picture of David is covered, but the picture of Jonathan is still visible. Talk about how even though Jonathan couldn't see David, he still loved his friend and thought of him all the time.

4. Let children affix a heart-shaped sticker to Jonathan's chest to remind them that Jonathan kept his friend David in his heart. Read the Scripture verse, and explain that to be *loyal* means to never forget your friends, even when they're far away.

Talk about:

Ask:
- What friends or family members live far away from you? How do you keep in touch with them?
- Why does God want us to remember our friends and family members who are far away?
- Today, how can you show your friends that you love them, even if they're far away?

Say: God wants us to remember that friends are loyal to each other all the time—even when they're far apart. Today, think of one way to share God's love with a friend or family member who is far away. Maybe you can draw a picture and send it to your friend.

Pray: God, thank you for our friends and family members. We know you love them no matter where they are. Help us to always remember our friends. In Jesus' name, amen.

"A friend is always loyal"

(Proverbs 17:17a).

Permission to photocopy this coloring page from *Coloring Creations 2: 52 New Bible Activity Pages* granted for local church use. Copyright © Group Publishing, Inc., 1515 Cascade Ave., Loveland, CO 80538. group.com

God's Power Helps Elijah and the Widow

1 Kings 17:1-24

What you need:

For each child...

• 1 copy of page 39

You'll also need...

• small crackers
• tan paper
• Coloring Creations Kit

What to do:

Write children's names on their pages. Cut tan paper into small rectangles. Set out crackers, glue, and crayons.

1. Give each child an activity page and a cracker. Let children think about how they'd feel if the cracker was the only food they had for the entire week. Have children set aside the crackers, and give each child a paper rectangle.

2. Direct children to glue the paper crackers to the picture of bread on their papers. As they color the papers, talk about how Elijah visited a woman and her son. The woman only had a tiny bit of food left...and Elijah asked if he could eat it!

3. Read the Scripture verse aloud, and tell children that Elijah believed that God was mighty and powerful, and that God would take care of them somehow.

4. Tell children that the woman fed Elijah everything she had, and the next morning, God had provided more food! Let children eat the crackers they set aside earlier.

Talk about:

Ask: • How did God help Elijah and the woman?

• How does God help us?

Say: The woman obeyed God and gave all the food she had to Elijah. When she did, she saw how powerful and mighty God is! He provided more food! Let's praise our mighty God.

Pray: Mighty God, we love you! Thank you for taking care of us in such amazing ways. We praise you because you are mighty and powerful. In Jesus' name, amen.

"O Lord...you are powerful and mighty"

(adapted from 2 Chronicles 20:6).

God Answers Elijah's Prayer

1 Kings 18:22-38

What you need:

For each child...

• 1 copy of page 41

You'll also need...

• blue glitter glue
• squares of yellow, orange, and red tissue paper
• Coloring Creations Kit

What to do:

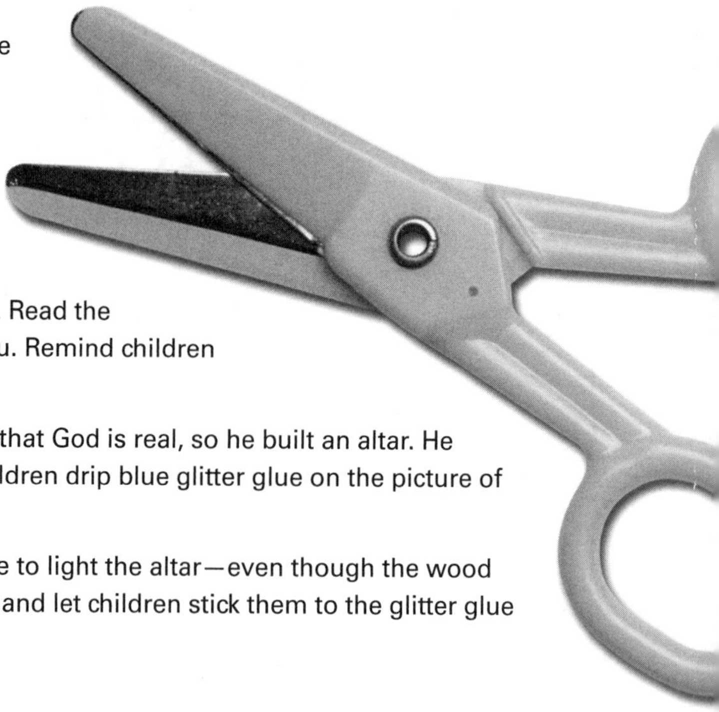

Write children's names on their pages. Set out blue glitter glue and crayons.

1. Give each child an activity page, and let children begin coloring the pictures.

2. Explain that people were following fake gods—worshiping idols that weren't real. Tell children that Elijah worshiped the one, true God. Read the Scripture verse, and have children say it with you. Remind children that we should only pray to the one, true God.

3. Talk about how Elijah wanted to show everyone that God is real, so he built an altar. He poured lots and lots of water on the altar. Let children drip blue glitter glue on the picture of the altar.

4. Say that Elijah prayed and asked God to send fire to light the altar—even though the wood was all wet. Hand out the pieces of tissue paper, and let children stick them to the glitter glue to show that God set the wet altar on fire!

Talk about:

Ask: • How did God answer Elijah's prayer?

• When is a time that God answered your prayers?

• How do you know that God is real?

Say: Elijah didn't want the people to worship fake gods—he wanted them to pray to and worship the one, true God! When God set the wet altar on fire, the people knew that there really is only one true God! Let's talk to our one true God right now.

Pray: God, you *are* real. You are mighty. Thank you for hearing us and answering our prayers. Help us to show others that you are the only true God. In Jesus' name, amen.

"But the Lord is the only true God"

(Jeremiah 10:10a).

Permission to photocopy this coloring page from *Coloring Creations 2: 52 New Bible Activity Pages* granted for local church use. Copyright © Group Publishing, Inc., 1515 Cascade Ave., Loveland, CO 80538. group.com

The Temple Is Repaired

2 Kings 22:1–23:3

What you need:

For each child...

• 1 copy of page 43

You'll also need...

• fine-grade sandpaper
• Coloring Creations Kit

What to do:

Write children's names on their pages. Cut fine-grade sandpaper into thin strips about 3 inches long and set them out, along with glue and markers.

1. Hand each child an activity page, and point to the pictures of the men building. Explain that the men are building the Temple—a building that was kind of like a church.

2. Let children use markers to color the picture, being careful to work hard and do their best. Talk about how the men were working hard to repair the Temple because it had been burned and torn down. Read the Scripture verse, and explain that the king, Josiah, wanted to make the Temple beautiful and strong again.

3. Show children how to glue the strips of sandpaper to the building, creating the strong timbers and wood that the men used.

4. When children finish, guide them in helping you clean up the craft area until it's spotless. Talk about ways we can take care of God's house.

Talk about:

Ask: • Why do you think the men wanted to rebuild the Temple?

• Why is it important to take care of God's house?

• How can we take good care of our church building?

Say: Josiah wanted to make the Temple a special place again, so he had his men work hard. When the Temple was fixed, it was beautiful! We can take care of our church, too, by keeping it clean and putting away our toys. The church is God's house, and we can take good care of it.

Pray: Dear God, thank you for our wonderful church building. We want it to be a place where people love to worship you. Use our hands to make this church a special place where people can learn more about you. In Jesus' name, amen.

"I was glad when they said to me, 'Let us go to the house of the Lord'"

(Psalm 122:1).

The Good Shepherd Gives His Sheep What They Need

Psalm 23

What you need:

For each child...

• 1 copy of page 45

You'll also need...

• green yarn
• watercolor paints
• cups of water
• paintbrushes
• Coloring Creations Kit

What to do:

Write children's names on their pages. Set out all of the supplies listed above.

1. Give each child an activity page. Read the Scripture verse, and have children repeat it with you. Explain that God is like a shepherd; he takes care of us—his sheep. Let children tell what a little lamb would need in order to live.

2. Hand out pieces of green yarn and safety scissors. Let children snip yarn "grass" and glue it onto the picture. Talk about how sheep eat grass. Have children discuss the good things God provides for us to eat.

3. Direct children to use blue watercolor paints to color the stream in the picture. Talk about the yummy things God gives us to drink.

4. While children color the shepherd, have them share the names of some of the people God has provided to love them, like parents, grandparents, and teachers.

Talk about:

Ask: • Why does God provide so many good things for us?

• How else is God like a shepherd, taking care of us?

• How does it make you feel to know that God loves you and takes care of you?

Say: In this picture, the lamb looks happy and safe. We can be happy and snuggle up close to God because we trust him to care for us. Let's pray and thank God for being our good shepherd.

Pray: Dear God, thank you for being like a good shepherd who takes such good care of us. Listen now as we share some things we're thankful for: (Let children take turns saying the name of a person or thing they're thankful for.) We know that these good gifts come from you. Thank you! In Jesus' name, amen.

"The Lord is my shepherd"

(Psalm 23:1a).

Daniel Keeps Praying

Daniel 6:11-15

What you need:

For each child...
- 1 copy of page 47
- 1 pencil

You'll also need...
- yellow construction paper
- pencils
- Coloring Creations Kit

What to do:

Write children's names on their pages. Cut yellow construction paper into strips (about 1/4x3-inches), and set them out along with glue, pencils, and colored pencils.

1. Give each child about 10 paper strips and one pencil. Demonstrate how to curl the paper around the pencil. Hold the paper in place for a few seconds then slip the pencil out. The paper will still be curly.

2. Have children curl each of their paper strips. As children hold the papers in place (around the pencil), have them say brief sentence prayers, thanking God for family members, pets, or naming specific friends.

3. Hand each child an activity page, and explain that Daniel loved to pray—he prayed three times every day. A king made a rule that said people couldn't pray to God anymore...if they did, they'd be thrown into a cave with lions! But that didn't stop Daniel from praying.

4. Let children glue their paper curls onto the lions' manes then color their pictures. Explain that God kept Daniel safe, even when Daniel was surrounded by lions. Tell children that God was glad Daniel kept praying. Read the Scripture verse, and have children repeat it. Explain that God wants us to pray to him all the time!

Talk about:

Ask:
- Why did Daniel want to keep praying, no matter what?
- When do you pray?
- What do you usually pray about?
- Why does God want us to always pray?

Say: Daniel loved talking to God—even if it meant he would get into trouble. God protected Daniel from the lions, and people learned that God is real. God wants us to always talk to him, just as Daniel did. Let's talk to God right now!

Pray: God, thank you for listening to us when we pray. We're so glad we can tell you anything. Help us to be brave like Daniel, and to never stop praying. In Jesus' name, amen.

"Never stop praying"

(1 Thessalonians 5:17).

Jonah Is Thrown Overboard

Jonah 1:4-17

What you need:

For each child...

- 1 copy of page 49

You'll also need...

- watercolor paints
- paintbrushes
- saltshakers filled with salt
- Coloring Creations Kit

What to do:

Write children's names on their pages. Set out crayons, watercolor paints, paintbrushes, and saltshakers.

1. Give each child an activity page. Allow children to color Jonah while you explain that Jonah was a man who listened to God...sometimes!

2. Let children color the boat as you talk about how God told Jonah to go to a city called Nineveh, to tell the people there to stop doing wrong things. Explain that Jonah was scared of the people in Nineveh so he didn't want to obey God. He jumped on a boat going away from Nineveh.

3. Guide children to color the men and the storm clouds. Tell how God sent a big storm that scared the sailors. Jonah knew that the storm was from God, so he said to throw him overboard and the storm would stop.

4. Let children use watercolor paints to color the sea and the big fish. Have children sprinkle salt over the watercolor, to make the salty ocean. Talk about how Jonah should have obeyed God. Read the Scripture verse, and talk about ways to love and obey God.

Talk about:

Ask:
- How do you think Jonah felt in the salty sea?
- Why didn't Jonah want to obey God?
- When is it hard for you to obey God?

Say: Jonah was afraid to talk to the people of Nineveh, but that was no reason to disobey God! Read the Scripture verse, and have children say it with you. **When God tells us to do something, he'll give us strength and take care of us as we obey. God took care of Jonah—even in the sea. Let's pray and ask God to help us obey.**

Pray: Dear God, we want to do what you say. Help us to open our ears, listen to you, and obey your words. In Jesus' name, amen.

"For I can do everything through Christ, who gives me strength"

(Philippians 4:13).

Jonah Prays to God Inside the Fish

Jonah 2:1-10

What you need:

For each child...
- 1 copy of page 51

You'll also need...
- wax paper
- spray bottle of water
- Coloring Creations Kit

What to do:

Write children's names on their pages. Cut or tear wax paper into pieces that are large enough to cover the picture of Jonah in the fish. You'll need one piece of wax paper per child. Set out crayons.

1. Spray the children lightly with water, and talk about how it feels to be wet. Then give each child an activity page.

2. Let children color the picture with crayons. Explain that God told Jonah to go to a city called Nineveh and tell the people there to stop doing wrong things. Instead of obeying, Jonah sailed far the other way. God sent a big storm, Jonah got thrown into the sea, and God sent a big fish to swallow him.

3. Have children tape a piece of wax paper over the picture of Jonah. Let them mist their pictures with water to see how God protected Jonah inside the fish. Read the Scripture verse. Tell children that Jonah was sad because he hadn't obeyed God. Jonah prayed to tell God he was sorry.

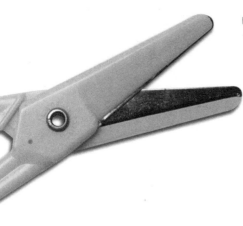

Talk about:

Ask:
- Why did Jonah pray inside the fish? What do you think he said?
- When is a time you disobeyed God or your parents? What happened?

Say: After Jonah told God he was sorry, God made the fish spit him out. Jonah was safe on dry land! He went straight to Nineveh and obeyed God. God wants us to obey him, too.

Pray: God, help us listen to obey you. Please keep us safe as we do what you ask us to do. We love you. In Jesus' name, amen.

"We must obey God"

(Acts 5:29a).

God's Promise

Isaiah 11:1-6; 35:3-10

What you need:

For each child...

- 1 copy of page 53
- 1 sheet of light-colored construction paper

You'll also need...

- Coloring Creations Kit

What to do:

Write children's names on their pages. Set out markers, glue, and construction paper.

1. Give each child an activity page, and ask what might happen if a lion and a lamb sat down to eat together. Explain that, in the Bible book of Isaiah, God promised that he would send a Messiah—Jesus—to save the world and help everyone get along with each other. Read the Scripture verse. Explain that God promised that when there was peace, even a lion and lamb would be friends.

2. Let children color the animals. Give each child a sheet of light-colored construction paper, and have kids glue their activity page to the construction paper to make a place mat.

3. Have children add happy faces to the border of their place mats as reminders that God promised that Jesus would bring joy and peace. Encourage children to use their place mats at home and to share God's promise with their families.

Talk about:

Ask: • How do you feel, knowing that Jesus will bring peace and help everyone get along?

• How do you think the world will be different when Jesus brings peace?

Say: God gave his people hope. He wanted them to know that it would be wonderful when Jesus came. He said that enemies would even sit down and eat together—like a lion sitting down with a lamb. Let's thank God for his promise.

Pray: God, thank you for sending Jesus to save us and bring peace. Help us tell others about Jesus so they can be happy, too. In Jesus' name, amen.

"In that day the wolf and the lamb will live together"

(Isaiah 11:6a).

The Angel Gabriel Comes to Mary

Luke 1:26-38

What you need:

For each child...

- 1 copy of page 55
- 2 wiggly eyes

You'll also need...

- glitter
- Coloring Creations Kit

What to do:

Write children's names on their pages. Set out glitter, crayons, wiggly eyes, glue, and glue sticks.

1. Give each child an activity page and two wiggly eyes. Explain that an angel visited a young woman named Mary. Read the Scripture verse to let kids know what the angel told Mary. Let children glue the wiggly eyes to Mary's eyes to show how surprised she was to see the angel and to hear his message.

2. Have children color the picture, being sure to color in the background, too. (This will make the angel stand out even more.)

3. Let children spread glue over the angel then carefully sprinkle a small amount of glitter over him. Talk about how surprised Mary must have been to see an angel!

Talk about:

Ask: • How do you think Mary felt when the angel visited her?

• What would you do if an angel visited you?

• When is a time someone told you good news?

Say: Mary must have been so surprised to see an angel—and then he told her she'd have a baby that would be the Son of God. Wow! What a surprise! God is good at giving us happy surprises. Think of one thing you're thankful God has given you. Let's thank God for those things right now.

Pray: Dear God, thank you for giving us these wonderful things. (Let children each say a thing they're thankful for.) In Jesus' name, amen.

"You will conceive and give birth to a son, and you will name him Jesus"

(Luke 1:31).

The Son of God Is Born!

Luke 2:1-7

What you need:

For each child...
- 1 copy of page 57

You'll also need...
- gift wrap
- Coloring Creations Kit

What to do:

Write children's names on their pages. Cut out 5-inch squares of gift wrap, and set out the squares along with markers, crayons, and tape.

1. Give each child an activity page, and let them color the picture.

2. Explain that Jesus is God's Son, who was born long ago to show God's love to us all. Tell children that Jesus is a special gift from God, then read the Scripture verse. Explain that when we believe in Jesus, God forgives the wrong things we do, and we can live with him forever.

3. Give each child a square of gift wrap, and let children tape the gift wrap over the baby Jesus. Direct children to just tape the gift wrap at the top, so they can lift up the paper to see the baby Jesus.

4. Sing a Christmas carol, such as "Silent Night" or "Away in a Manger" to thank God for sending the best gift ever—his Son, Jesus.

Talk about:

Ask:
- Why do you think God sent Jesus?
- Why is it so important to believe in Jesus?

Say: God sent Jesus to take away our sins, so we could live with God forever. That's what makes Jesus such a wonderful gift. As you open gifts at Christmas or your birthday, always remember that Jesus is the best gift ever!

Pray: God, thank you for sending Jesus. We know you love us a lot. Help us tell others about the greatest gift of all—Jesus. In Jesus' name, amen.

"Christ Jesus came into the world to save sinners"

(1 Timothy 1:15b).

Angels Announce Jesus' Birth to Shepherds

Luke 2:8-14

What you need:

For each child...

• 1 copy of page 59

You'll also need...

• cotton balls
• tinsel
• Coloring Creations Kit

What to do:

Write children's names on their pages. Set out tinsel, cotton balls, glue, and crayons.

1. Give each child an activity page. Point to the shepherds, and explain that one night, these shepherds were taking care of their sleepy sheep. Let children glue cotton balls to the sheep.

2. Tell children that it was late at night and the sky was dark. Have children color the sky with dark colors.

3. Say that suddenly a whole bunch of angels appeared in the sky. Read the Scripture verse to let children know what the angels said. Explain that the angels told the shepherds that God's Son, Jesus, had been born! Then the angels sang to the shepherds, praising God. Let children glue tinsel to the angels and the stars to show how beautiful they must have looked in the night sky.

4. Tell children that the shepherds went to worship God's Son, Jesus.

Talk about:

Ask: • What do you suppose the shepherds said to each other when they saw the angels?

• Who can you tell about Jesus?

Say: Instead of sending out birth announcements like we do today, God sent singing angels to tell people about Jesus' birth. That's cool! We can be just as cool by telling people about Jesus. Let's ask God to help us.

Pray: Dear God, thank you for sending Jesus to save us. Help us tell everyone we know about Jesus! In Jesus' name, amen.

"I bring you good news that will bring great joy to all people"

(from Luke 2:10).

The Parable of the Sower

Luke 8:4-15

What you need:

For each child...
• 1 copy of page 61

You'll also need...
• seeds
• Coloring Creations Kit

What to do:

Write children's names on their pages. Set out seeds, markers, and glue.

1. Give each child an activity page. As children color the page, explain that Jesus told a story about a person planting seeds.

2. Tell children that some of the seeds landed on rocky dirt and couldn't grow. Some seeds were eaten by birds and couldn't grow. Some of the seeds started to grow, but weeds grew around them and the seeds couldn't grow.

3. Let children spread glue on the pictures of the seeds, then sprinkle seeds on the glue. Say that some seeds were planted in good, healthy soil, and they grew and grew and grew!

4. Read the Scripture verse. Explain that a disciple is someone who loves and follows Jesus. Say that we should tell people about Jesus, so their love for him can grow—just like seeds!

Talk about:

Ask: • Who can you tell about Jesus?

• What will you say about Jesus?

• Why is it important to tell people about Jesus?

Say: When we tell people about Jesus, they can believe in him and live with him in heaven someday. By telling others about Jesus, we can help their love for him grow and grow...like a seed in good dirt! We never have to be afraid or embarrassed to tell others about Jesus. Read the Scripture verse, and have children repeat it. **We need to share the good news about Jesus! Let's pray for people who don't know Jesus.**

Pray: God, we want everyone to know and love Jesus. Listen as we share the names of people who need to know about Jesus. (Let children each say the name of someone they want to tell about Jesus.) **Please help us tell these people about Jesus. In Jesus' name, amen.**

"For I am not ashamed of this Good News about Christ"

(Romans 1:16a).

Jesus Heals Jairus' Daughter

Luke 8:40-42, 49-56

What you need:

For each child...

• 1 copy of page 63

You'll also need...

• scraps of cloth
• Coloring Creations Kit

What to do:

Write children's names on their pages. Set out safety scissors, scraps of cloth, glue, and crayons.

1. Give each child an activity page. Let children color the picture. Tell children that the girl was very sick, but Jesus made her well.

2. Let children feel the cloth and talk about how soft and good it feels. Read the Scripture verse. Say that Jesus is always with us, even when we're sick or sad.

3. Let children cut the cloth into small pieces (about 1 inch) and glue them to the blanket like a quilt.

Talk about:

Ask: • Who takes care of you when you're sick?

• How does it feel to know that Jesus is always with you?

• How can you thank Jesus for taking care of you?

Say: Jesus was with the little girl and healed her. Jesus is always with us. That doesn't mean you'll never get sick or hurt—but it does mean that Jesus will always be with you to help and comfort you.

Pray: God, thank you for always being with us when we're sad. We're glad that you cover us with your love all the time. In Jesus' name, amen.

"I am with you always"

(Matthew 28:20b).

Permission to photocopy this coloring page from *Coloring Creations 2:
52 New Bible Activity Pages* granted for local church use. Copyright ©
Group Publishing, Inc., 1515 Cascade Ave., Loveland, CO 80538. group.com

The Parable of the Lost Son

Luke 15:11-32

What you need:

For each child...

- 1 copy of page 65
- 1cup of chocolate pudding
- 1 plastic spoon

You'll also need...

- a few cups of diluted brown tempera paint
- cotton swabs
- Coloring Creations Kit

ALLERGY ALERT

What to do:

Write children's names on their pages. Set out cups of diluted paint, cotton swabs, and crayons.

1. Give each child an activity page. Let children begin coloring the picture.

2. Explain that Jesus told a story about a boy who ran away from home, even though his father loved him very much. The boy ran out of money and got a job feeding stinky, dirty pigs.

3. Let children use cotton swabs to spread a thin layer of brown paint on the pigs, the boy, and the ground.

4. Tell children that the boy finally went home, and his father forgave him. In fact, the father threw a big party for his son. Give each child a cup of pudding to eat to celebrate the father's forgiveness. Read the Scripture verse, and talk about the sweetness of God's love and forgiveness.

Talk about:

Ask:
- Why do you think the father forgave his son?
- Why does God forgive us?
- Who do *you* need to forgive?

Say: Jesus told this story to teach people that God loves them and will forgive their sins. Jesus wants us to forgive others, too. Remember how sweet the pudding tasted? Forgiveness is sweet, too!

Pray: Dear God, thank you for loving us enough to forgive our sins. Help us to forgive others. In Jesus' name, amen.

"O Lord, you are so good, so ready to forgive"

(Psalm 86:5a).

Zacchaeus Wants to See Jesus

Luke 19:1-4

What you need:

For each child...
- 1 copy of page 67
- 1 craft stick

You'll also need...
- imitation leaves (or you can cut some from green construction paper)
- Coloring Creations Kit

What to do:

Write children's names on their pages. Cut Zacchaeus from each picture, then set out markers, imitation leaves, and glue or tape.

1. Give each child a picture of Zacchaeus. While children color Zacchaeus, explain that he was a man who sometimes cheated others out of money. Zacchaeus heard that Jesus was coming to town, and he wanted to see Jesus. Let children glue or tape Zacchaeus to a craft stick.

2. Give each child an activity page, and let children color the picture of Jesus. Direct children to the leaves, and let them glue the leaves to the tree, covering the hole where you've cut out Zacchaeus.

3. Explain that Zacchaeus was too short to see over the crowds of people, so he climbed up a tree. Show children how to make Zacchaeus "climb" up the tree so he can see Jesus.

Talk about:

Ask: • Why do you think Zacchaeus wanted to see Jesus?

• Why is it important to know Jesus?

Say: Zacchaeus knew he needed to see Jesus. And once he got to know Jesus, Zacchaeus wanted to stop doing wrong things. Knowing Jesus is the only way to be forgiven for the wrong things we do. Listen to what the Bible says. Read the Scripture verse. **Let's thank God right now for sending Jesus to help us do right!**

Pray: Wonderful God, we love you and thank you for Jesus. Help us to get to know him better every day. In Jesus' name, amen.

"Jesus told him, 'I am the way, the truth, and the life' "

(John 14:6a).

Zaccheus Is Sorry

Luke 19:8

What you need:

For each child...

• 1 copy of page 69

You'll also need...

• aluminum foil
• Coloring Creations Kit

What to do:

Write children's names on their pages. Set out foil, safety scissors, glue, and markers.

1. Give each child a piece of aluminum foil. Let children tear off pieces of foil and shape them into coins.

2. Give children their activity pages. Point to the picture of sad Zaccheus, and explain that Zaccheus was sorry he had taken money from people. Tell children that Jesus helped Zaccheus know that he'd done wrong.

3. Let children glue their foil money in Zaccheus' bags. Then allow children to color the picture of Jesus and Zaccheus.

Talk about:

Ask: • What had Zaccheus done wrong?

• How do you feel when you've done something wrong?

• What should you do when you've done something wrong?

Say: Jesus helped Zaccheus see that taking money from people was a bad thing to do. Then Zaccheus felt sorry and sad. He wanted to do what was right. Jesus helped Zaccheus do right, and he'll help us, too. Listen to what the Bible says. Read the Scripture verse, and have children repeat it with you. **The Bible says to do right, and Jesus will help us!**

Pray: Dear God, we want to please you and do right. Help us to know right from wrong and to make good choices. Thank you for Jesus, who shows us the right thing to do. In Jesus' name, amen.

"Do what is right and good in the Lord's sight"

(Deuteronomy 6:18a).

Permission to photocopy this coloring page from *Coloring Creations 2: 52 New Bible Activity Pages* granted for local church use. Copyright © Group Publishing, Inc., 1515 Cascade Ave., Loveland, CO 80538. group.com

Zaccheus Does What's Right

Luke 19:9-10

What you need:

For each child...
- 1 copy of page 71
- 1 large paper cup

You'll also need...
- yellow construction paper
- Coloring Creations Kit

What to do:

Write children's names on their pages. Cut a 2-inch horizontal slit in each page, just above the pile of coins between Zaccheus and the people. Set out crayons or markers, transparent tape, cups, and safety scissors.

1. Hand out sheets of yellow paper, and help children cut out 1-inch paper coins. (You may need to help younger preschoolers with this step, or cut the coins ahead of time.)

2. Tell children that in the Bible, a man named Zaccheus loved money and took money from people. He was a tax collector, and he always made people pay too much. Tell children that Jesus helped Zaccheus discover that he was doing wrong.

3. Give each child an activity page. Let children color the picture of Zaccheus and the people. Read the Scripture verse, and explain that Zaccheus gave back all the money— and even more! Say that Jesus helped Zaccheus do what was right.

4. Help children each curl their pages around a cup and tape the paper to the cup. The picture will extend above the rim of the cup. Let children slip the paper coins into the slit, so they drop into the cup.

Talk about:

Ask: • How did Zaccheus learn to do what's right?

• What things can you do that would make Jesus happy?

• Who helps us do what's right?

Say: Jesus helped Zaccheus do the right thing. He gave money back to the people, and I'll bet it made the people so happy! I *know* it made God happy. Each time you add a coin to your picture, think of a way you can do something right. That will make God happy!

Pray: Dear God, we love doing things that make you happy. Show us how to do right every day. Help us do right even when it might be hard. In Jesus' name, amen.

"Never get tired of doing good"

(2 Thessalonians 3:13b).

Jesus Raises Lazarus

John 11:1-45

What you need:

For each child...

- 1 copy of page 73
- 4 wiggly eyes

You'll also need...

- white facial tissues
- Coloring Creations Kit

What to do:

Write children's names on their pages. Set out wiggly eyes, facial tissues, glue, and crayons.

1. Give each child an activity page and a tissue. Tell children that the man walking toward Jesus was named Lazarus—he was a good friend of Jesus'.

2. Direct children to fold back the part of the picture with Lazarus on it, so that Lazarus isn't showing. Explain that while Jesus was in another town, Lazarus died. Have children turn the pages over so they can see Lazarus. Let children tear strips of tissue and glue them over Lazarus. Talk about how in Bible times, people were wrapped in strips of cloth when they died.

3. Let children turn their papers over so the picture of Jesus, Martha, and Mary is showing. While children color the picture, explain that when Jesus heard that Lazarus died, he came right away. Jesus visited with Lazarus' sisters, Mary and Martha. Then Jesus did something surprising!

4. Tell children that Jesus went to the place where Lazarus was buried and called, "Lazarus! Lazarus!" And after Jesus called him, Lazarus was alive again! Let children unfold their pictures so Lazarus is showing.

5. Have kids glue wiggly eyes to Mary and Martha to show how surprised they were that Jesus had made Lazarus alive again. Read the Scripture verse, and let children repeat it. Explain that Jesus can do anything!

Talk about:

Ask:
- **How did Jesus surprise Lazarus, Mary, and Martha?**
- **Do you think there's anything that Jesus can't do? Explain.**
- **Jesus is amazing! Who can you tell about Jesus this week?**

Say: Mary and Martha were sad—they thought they'd never see their brother again. But Jesus raised Lazarus from the dead. Jesus promises to always be with us and to give us a home in heaven. Let's pray and thank God for sending Jesus.

Pray: Lord, we thank you for sending Jesus. We thank you for his amazing power. Thank you for offering us your love and a home in heaven! In Jesus' name, amen.

"For nothing is impossible with God"

(Luke 1:37).

Permission to photocopy this coloring page from *Coloring Creations 2: 52 New Bible Activity Pages* granted for local church use. Copyright © Group Publishing, Inc., 1515 Cascade Ave., Loveland, CO 80538. group.com

The Miraculous Catch of Fish

John 21:1-13

What you need:

For each child...

- 1 copy of page 75
- a handful of colored fish-shaped crackers

ALLERGY ALERT

You'll also need...

- colored construction paper
- plastic netting
- Coloring Creations Kit

What to do:

Write children's names on their pages. Cut the netting into 4x6-inch pieces. Cut or tear small paper fish from the colored paper. Set out glue, markers, netting, and paper fish.

1. Give each child a piece of netting, and tell them that Jesus' friends were fishermen who caught fish in nets. Explain that one day, the men hadn't caught any fish—they were sad!

2. Tell children that Jesus told his friends to put their nets into the water on the other side of the boat. When the men obeyed, their nets became full of fish! Hand children each a handful of paper fish, and let them place the fish in their "fishing nets" so they're full.

3. Hand out the activity pages, and let children color the picture. Read the Scripture verse, and explain that the verse is talking about Jesus' miracles. Say that a miracle is something amazing that only God can do. Talk about some of the other miracles Jesus did. Let children glue the fishing net to the picture of the net. Then let children enjoy a treat of fish crackers as they discuss these questions.

Talk about:

Ask:
- How do you think Jesus' friends felt when they saw all those fish?
- Why do you think Jesus did miracles?

Say: Jesus did many amazing miracles while he was on earth. He wanted to show people God's incredible power and love. Listen to what the Bible says. Read the Scripture. Every time we think of one of Jesus' miracles, we can remember that he is the Son of God!

Pray: Mighty God, your power amazes us! Thank you for sending Jesus, and thank you for his miracles. Help us to tell others that Jesus is the Son of God! In Jesus' name, amen.

"But these are written so that you may continue to believe that Jesus is the Messiah, the Son of God"

(John 20:31a).

Permission to photocopy this coloring page from *Coloring Creations 2: 52 New Bible Activity Pages* granted for local church use. Copyright © Group Publishing, Inc., 1515 Cascade Ave., Loveland, CO 80538. group.com

Jesus and His Followers Share a Meal

Luke 22:7-19

What you need:

For each child...

• 1 copy of page 77

ALLERGY ALERT

You'll also need...

• brown craft foam
• red or purple watercolor paints
• paintbrushes
• cups for rinsing brushes
• Coloring Creations Kit

What to do:

Write children's names on their pages. Cut the craft foam into small rectangles. Set out crayons, craft foam pieces, glue, watercolors, brushes, and cups of water.

1. Give each child an activity page. Point to the picture, and explain that Jesus shared a special meal with his friends. Let children color Jesus and the two friends.

2. Hand out slices of craft-foam "bread," and explain that, as part of the meal, Jesus and his friends had bread. Tell children that Jesus broke the bread and gave some to his friends. Jesus told his friends that whenever they had this special meal, they should remember Jesus.

3. Let children glue the craft foam pieces to the bread in the picture. Be sure they glue a piece to each of the disciples' hands, too. Encourage children to say the Scripture verse, "Do this to remember me," as they glue the pieces.

4. Tell children that Jesus and his friends had something to drink with their meal. Allow children to use purple or red watercolor paints to color the drink in the cup. Let them repeat the Scripture as they color the cups.

Talk about:

Ask: • Why did Jesus want his friends to remember him?

• What makes you think about Jesus?

Say: Jesus wants us to remember him during the special meal we just learned about. But he wants us to think about him at other times, too! Jesus wants us to remember how much he loves us and that he wants to be our friend forever. Let's talk to our friend Jesus right now.

Pray: Precious Jesus, we love you. We love to think about you and to remember how much you love us. Please be with us as we play, sleep, and eat. Thank you for loving us. In Jesus' name, amen.

"Do this to remember me"

(Luke 22:19b).

Jesus Prays in the Garden

Mark 14:27-50

What you need:

For each child...

- 1 copy of page 79
- 1 green crayon

You'll also need...

- green construction paper
- leaves (real or imitation)
- safety scissors
- Coloring Creations Kit

What to do:

Write children's names on their pages. Peel the wrappers from the green crayons. Set out construction paper, green crayons, glue sticks, and markers.

1. Give each child a sheet of green construction paper, a green crayon, and a handful of leaves. Let children lay the leaves in front of them and place the green construction paper over the leaves. Demonstrate how to lay a crayon on the paper and rub over the paper to get a leaf design on the paper.

2. Hand each child his or her activity page, and let children color the picture of Jesus. Tell children that Jesus went to a quiet place—a garden—to pray. Say that Jesus wanted to be alone with God. Read the Scripture verse, and talk about times when praying makes us feel better.

3. Let children tear or cut leaf shapes from the green construction papers. Direct children to add glue to one end of each leaf shape, and then glue the leaves so they cover Jesus. Children should be able to gently pull back the leaves to see Jesus praying.

Talk about:

Ask: • Why do you think Jesus went into the garden to pray?

• Where do you usually pray?

• Why do you feel better when you talk to God?

Say: Jesus was sad because he knew he would be going through a hard time. So he wanted to be alone with God, to talk to him about it. We can talk to God, too—anytime and anywhere. In fact, let's talk to God right now.

Pray: Dear God, you are so mighty and powerful, loving, and kind. We feel better when we talk to you, knowing that you hear us and are with us. Help us be brave when we're facing hard times. Thank you for loving us and being with us all the time. In Jesus' name, amen.

"You should pray"

(James 5:13b).

Permission to photocopy this coloring page from *Coloring Creations 2: 52 New Bible Activity Pages* granted for local church use. Copyright © Group Publishing, Inc., 1515 Cascade Ave., Loveland, CO 80538. group.com

Peter Denies Jesus

Mark 14:53-72; 15:21-41

What you need:

For each child...
- 1 copy of page 81

You'll also need...
- Coloring Creations Kit
- ruler

What to do:

Write children's names on their pages. Draw a line from the bottom of the page, just to the left of Peter, straight up, ending just above Peter's head. Then continue the line to the right, over Peter's head. (If you have mostly 3-year-olds, go ahead and cut along the line.) Set out crayons and safety scissors.

1. Give each child an activity page. Explain that this is Peter, a good friend of Jesus'. Tell children that Jesus had been arrested for telling people about God. Let children color the picture of Peter.

2. Help children cut along the line you made and fold the picture of Peter so his back is to the children.

3. Have children color the rooster. Explain that Jesus had told Peter that Peter would say he didn't even know Jesus. In fact, Peter would say he didn't know Jesus three times before the rooster crowed twice.

4. Let children use their pictures to act out the story. Every time Peter denies Christ, have children fold their picture so Peter's back is turned. Talk about how Peter turned his back on Jesus because Peter was afraid.

Talk about:

Ask: • Why did Peter say he didn't know Jesus?

• Have you ever been afraid to say that you know Jesus? Why or why not?

• How can you bravely tell people that you know and love Jesus?

Say: Peter was afraid he'd get in trouble if he said he knew Jesus. We don't have to be afraid—we should tell everyone we know about Jesus! Here's what the Bible says. Read the Scripture verse. Explain that it's important to tell others that Jesus is Lord. Now let's sing a special prayer about knowing that Jesus is Lord!

Teach children this prayer to the tune of "Jesus Loves Me."

> Jesus, you are Lord, I know.
> For the Bible tells me so.
> You love me and I love you.
> I want my friends to love you, too.
> Jesus is Lord!
> Jesus is Lord!
> Jesus is Lord!
> I want my friends to know.

"And every tongue confess that Jesus Christ is Lord, to the glory of God the Father"

(Philippians 2:11).

Jesus' Crucifixion

Matthew 27:11-56

What you need:

For each child...
- 1 copy of page 83

You'll also need...
- spray bottle of water
- wooden coffee stirrers
- Coloring Creations Kit

What to do:

Write children's names on their pages. Cut the coffee stirrers into segments a few inches long to be glued to the crosses in the picture. Set out the segments, markers, glue, and spray bottle. Be sure to set the spray bottle to "mist."

1. Give each child a coloring page, and explain that Jesus died on a cross.

2. Let children glue the coffee stirrer segments over the crosses. Read the Scripture verse, and have children repeat it with you. Say that Jesus died on a cross to take the punishment for the wrong things we do.

3. Have children color the picture with markers, being sure to color the sky and clouds.

4. Let children take turns spraying their pictures lightly with the spray bottle. As the colors run, talk about how sad Jesus' friends were. Have children imagine that the picture is crying, just like Jesus' friends.

Talk about:

Ask:
- How does it make you feel to know that Jesus died on the cross for you?
- How can you thank Jesus for giving his life for you?

Say: This story makes us sad, thinking about how much it hurt Jesus to die on the cross. The happy part of the story is that Jesus didn't stay dead! He rose from the dead three days later! We can celebrate and praise God for his amazing love for us.

Pray: We praise you, God, for sending Jesus to die for us. We praise you because Jesus rose again. Thank you for sending Jesus! In Jesus' name, amen.

"Christ died for our sins"

(1 Corinthians 15:3b).

Permission to photocopy this coloring page from *Coloring Creations 2: 52 New Bible Activity Pages* granted for local church use. Copyright © Group Publishing, Inc., 1515 Cascade Ave., Loveland, CO 80538. group.com

The Tomb Is Empty

Mark 16:1-8

What you need:

For each child...

- 1 copy of page 85
- 2 small paper plates

You'll also need...

- stapler
- pebbles
- Coloring Creations Kit

What to do:

Write children's names on their pages. Set out crayons, pebbles, safety scissors, and plates.

1. Give each child an activity page and two plates. Help children set one plate over the picture and trace around it. Guide children in cutting out the circle.

2. While children color their pictures, point out the women and tell children that these women were friends of Jesus. The women were sad that Jesus had died, so they went to visit the tomb where Jesus' body was.

3. Point to the angel, and explain that when the women got to the tomb, it was empty, and an angel was there. The angel told the women that Jesus wasn't dead anymore—he'd risen from the dead! The women were excited and happy.

4. Read the Scripture verse, and tell children that we can shout with joy because Jesus is alive today. Help children glue their activity page "circles" to the backside of one of the plates.

5. Let children turn over the plate and put a handful of pebbles on the plate. Turn over another plate, and place it on top of the first plate. Staple around the rim of both plates, trapping the pebbles inside. Show children how to use their noisemakers to shout with joy to the Lord, celebrating that Jesus is alive!

Talk about:

Ask: • Why were the women in this Bible story so happy?

• How can we celebrate the good news that Jesus is alive?

Say: The women were surprised and happy because Jesus was alive. We can be happy, too—and we can share that happiness with others. I want to tell God right now how incredible it is that Jesus is alive. Then we can shake our noisemakers as soon as I say, "amen."

Pray: Amazing God, you surprise us and make us so happy! Thank you for giving Jesus the power to rise from the dead. In Jesus' name, amen. Lead children in cheering and shaking their noisemakers.

"Shout with joy to the Lord"

(Psalm 100:1a).

Jesus Is Alive!

John 20:1-9

What you need:

For each child...
- 1 copy of page 87
- 1 small cup

You'll also need...
- gray construction paper
- Coloring Creations Kit

What to do:

Write children's names on their pages. Set out gray construction paper, transparent tape, markers, and small cups. Carefully cut out the black part of the tomb on each picture.

1. Tell children that Jesus, God's Son, came to live on earth. While Jesus was on earth, he taught people about God's love and showed them God's love. Then some people hurt and killed Jesus because they didn't believe he was God.

2. Explain that three days after Jesus died, his friends went to visit the tomb where Jesus had been put. Give each child an activity page, and ask them what they notice about the cave or tomb. Tell children that Jesus rose from the dead. Explain that Jesus did that so we could be friends with God. Jesus died to take away our sins so we could live with God forever!

3. Let children color the pages. Then help each child tape the open side of a small cup to the cave entrance (from the back of the page) to create an empty tomb. Lead children in saying the Scripture verse. Let children tell each other the good news that Jesus is alive. One partner can ask, "Where's Jesus?" The other can repeat the Scripture verse. Then they'll switch roles.

4. Then allow each child to each tear a round shape from gray paper and glue the "stone" near the tomb entrance. Talk about how the heavy stone had been rolled away so everyone could see that Jesus wasn't in the tomb—he was alive!

Talk about:

Ask: • Why do you think Jesus died for you and then rose again?

• How can you thank Jesus for taking away your sins?

Say: Jesus took the punishment for our sins—the wrong things we do that make God so sad. When we believe in Jesus, our sins are forgiven and we can be friends with God...forever! Let's pray and thank God that he raised Jesus from the dead.

Pray: Dear God, we're so glad that the tomb was empty that morning. Thank you for loving us so much that you let Jesus die to take away our sins. Thank you for raising Jesus from the dead. We love you. In Jesus' name, amen.

"He isn't here! He is risen from the dead"

(Matthew 28:6a).

The Road to Emmaus

Luke 24:13-35

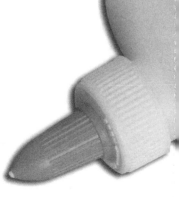

What you need:

For each child…

- 1 copy of page 89
- 3 twigs
- a handful of thin pretzel sticks

ALLERGY ALERT

You'll also need…

- tempera paint (any color)
- paper plate
- wet wipes
- Coloring Creations Kit

What to do:

Write children's names on their pages. Set out markers, a plate of tempera paint, and wet wipes.

1. Give each child an activity sheet and three twigs. Tell children that two men were walking along a road a few days after Jesus had died and risen again. Have children glue the twigs to the men's walking sticks in the picture. Then let each child dip two fingertips in the paint and "walk" his or her fingers along the road.

2. Clean children's hands, and let them color the picture. Explain that as the men walked, Jesus joined them—but the men didn't recognize him at first. The men talked about all the amazing things Jesus had done. They told how he had been killed and how he'd risen from the dead.

3. Tell children that Jesus and the men came to a town and got something to eat. Let children snap a few pretzel sticks and eat them. Explain that as soon as Jesus broke bread to eat with the men, they realized that it was Jesus.

4. While children eat the rest of their pretzels, read the Scripture verse and talk about how we can follow Jesus, just as the men in the picture did.

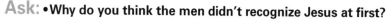

Talk about:

Ask: • Why do you think the men didn't recognize Jesus at first?

• What are some things you don't understand about Jesus?

• Who can help you understand more about Jesus?

Say: The men didn't realize that it was Jesus, even though they walked with him a while. Even though we love Jesus, there are times we just don't understand everything about him. But God has given you grown-ups in your life who want to help you understand more about Jesus. And you can always talk to God and ask him your questions, too. Let's pray and ask God to help us know more about Jesus.

Pray: Dear God, thank you for sending Jesus. We know that you want us to follow him. Help us to know Jesus better every day. In Jesus' name, amen.

"Follow in his steps"

(1 Peter 2:21b).

Jesus Forgives Peter

John 21:4-17

What you need:

For each child...

- 1 copy of page 91
- 1 facial tissue

You'll also need...

- watercolor paints
- paintbrushes
- black crayons
- cups of water
- yellow and orange tissue paper
- Coloring Creations Kit

What to do:

Write children's names on their pages. Set out squares of yellow and orange tissue paper, glue, paints and paintbrushes, cups of water, tissues, and black crayons.

1. Give each child his or her activity page. Tell children that when Jesus was arrested, Peter was afraid to admit that he knew Jesus. Peter said that he didn't know Jesus—even though he was one of Jesus' best friends. Let children color Peter's robe black to show how sad and dark Peter felt, knowing that he'd said he didn't know Jesus.

2. Let children color the water with blue watercolor paints. As children paint, tell them that one day, Peter was out fishing with his brother and friends. Jesus had risen from the dead, and he came to the beach and made a fire. Let children glue tissue paper flames to the fire.

3. Tell children that Jesus made a breakfast of fish for Peter. Then he told Peter that he forgave Peter for saying those things. Jesus washed away the wrong things Peter had said and done—he wasn't angry with Peter.

4. Give each child a white facial tissue, and have children glue the tissue over the black crayon markings to make Peter's robe look new and clean. Explain that when we believe in Jesus, our hearts are made new and clean because our sins are forgiven.

Talk about:

Ask: • How do you feel when you've done something wrong?

• Tell about a time when someone forgave you. How did that feel?

• Why is it hard to forgive the way Jesus forgives us?

Say: Jesus forgave Peter and showed us what it means to forgive. When someone has said something mean or hurt our feelings, it's hard to say, "I forgive you." But that's just what Jesus wants us to do! Listen to what the Bible says. Read the Scripture verse, and have children repeat it. Let's pray and ask Jesus to help us be forgiving, just like he is.

Pray: Lord, we're so thankful that you forgive us when we do wrong things. Help us remember Jesus and forgive others like he forgives us. We love you. In Jesus' name, amen.

"Forgive others, and you will be forgiven"

(Luke 6:37b).

Jesus Rises to Heaven

Matthew 28:16-20; Acts 1:6-11

What you need:

For each child...

• 1 copy of page 93

You'll also need...

• white glue
• measuring cup
• white shaving cream
• paintbrushes
• glitter
• Coloring Creations Kit

What to do:

Write children's names on their pages. Make foam paint by mixing 1 cup of white glue with 1 cup of shaving cream. Allow the mixture to sit for a few minutes before kids use it.

1. Give each child an activity page. Set out the foam paint, paintbrushes, glitter, and crayons. While children color the picture of Jesus and the sky, explain that Jesus came to earth to show God's love and to teach people about God.

2. Tell children that after Jesus died, he rose from the dead. Then it was time for Jesus to go back to heaven and be with his father, God. Explain that Jesus' friends watched him rise up into the sky.

3. Let children paint the clouds with the foam paint. Read the Scripture verse, and tell children that Jesus told his friends, the disciples, to keep telling people about God's love. Jesus said to make everyone a disciple, or follower, of Jesus!

4. Direct children to sprinkle glitter on the foam paint as a reminder of how special Jesus is and how special our home in heaven will be if we believe in Jesus.

Talk about:

Ask: • What can you tell *me* about Jesus?

• Why does Jesus want us to tell others about him?

Say: If I tell (name of child in class) **about Jesus, and he** (or she) **tells** (name of another child in class), **and that person tells someone else...pretty soon the whole world might know about Jesus! Let's pray and say the names of people we want to tell about Jesus.**

Pray: **Dear God, thank you for sending Jesus to show us your wonderful love. Help us remember to tell these people about Jesus, so they can know about your love...**(Guide children in saying the names of people they want to tell about Jesus.) **In Jesus' name, amen.**

"Therefore, go and make disciples of all the nations"

(Matthew 28:19a).

The Holy Spirit Comes at Pentecost

Acts 2:1-13, 38-41

What you need:

For each child…
• 1 copy of page 95

You'll also need…
• red, yellow, and orange curling ribbon
• Coloring Creations Kit

What to do:

Write children's names on their pages. Curl strips of curling ribbon, and cut the curled ribbon into 3-inch pieces. Set out the curling ribbon strips, glue sticks, and crayons.

1. Give each child an activity page. Point to the men in the picture, and explain that in the Bible some people were talking about God's love. But other people didn't understand because they spoke a different language. Direct children to color each man a different color, as a reminder that the men spoke different languages.

2. Tell children that all of a sudden, a big wind blew through the room, and something that looked like fire appeared over the men's heads. Let children glue pieces of curling ribbon on the flames. Show children how to blow the ribbons to make the "flames" move!

3. Explain that the flames showed that God had sent a helper, called the Holy Spirit, to help the people. Suddenly everyone could understand what the men were saying! Lots of people heard about Jesus that day because of the Holy Spirit.

4. Read the Scripture verse aloud to each child, filling in the child's name for the word "you."

Talk about:

Ask:
• **Have you ever heard someone speak a different language? What was that like?**

• **Who helps you understand God's Word, the Bible?**

• **What is it like to know that God is always with you?**

Say: God helped his followers do great things. He was with them all the time, even when they couldn't see him. God is with us, too. God sent his Holy Spirit to help you and me tell others about Jesus. God is with us right now, so let's talk to God!

Pray: Dear God, thank you for sending your Holy Spirit to be with us all the time. Thank you for helping us tell others about Jesus. We love you so much! It's good to know you're always with us. In Jesus' name, amen.

"And be sure of this: I am with you always, even to the end of the age"

(Matthew 28:20b).

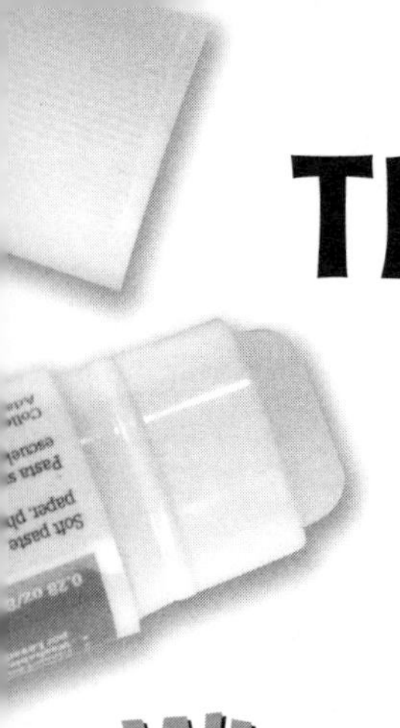

The Early Christians Share

Acts 2:42-47; 4:32-37

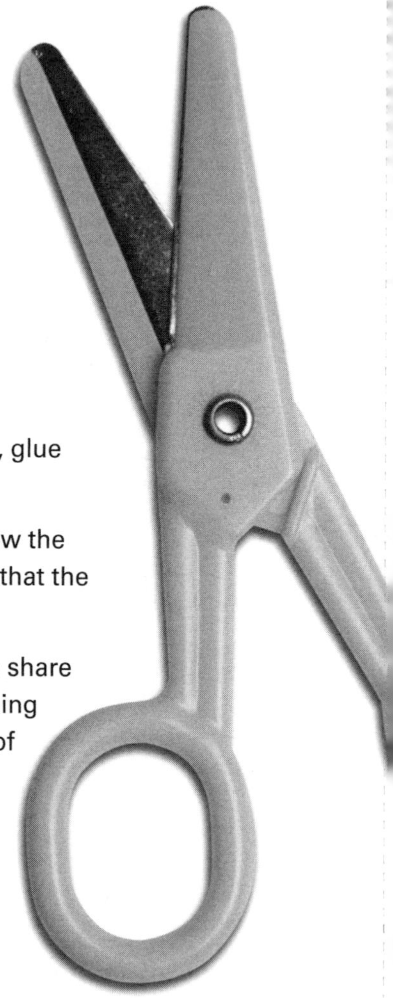

What you need:

For each child...

- 1 copy of page 97

You'll also need...

- old magazines
- Coloring Creations Kit

What to do:

Write children's names on their pages. Set out old magazines, safety scissors, glue sticks, and markers.

1. Give each child an activity page. While children color the picture, explain how the people in the picture are sharing with each other. Say that the Bible tells us that the first Christians helped each other by sharing food, money, and clothes.

2. Read the Scripture verse, and let children repeat it. Talk about things we can share with people who are in need. Let children cut pictures of toys, food, or clothing from the magazines. You might also encourage children to cut out pictures of people smiling or hugging, since we can always share love!

3. Let children glue the magazine pictures around the edge of their activity pages to create a frame. Tell children to point to one of the items they cut out, and encourage them to give that item to someone this week.

Talk about:

Ask: • How do you feel when friends share things with you?

• Why is it sometimes hard to share?

• Why do you think God wants us to share with people?

Say: When the Christians in the Bible shared things, they showed other people what God's love was like. We can do that today! When you share a toy, a smile, or your snack with a friend—you're helping them understand how good God's love feels. Let's share hugs with our friends right now while we pray. Have children join in a group hug while you pray.

Pray: Loving God, your love *does* feel so good to us. We want others to know that feeling, too. Show us each day how we can share a smile, a hug, a toy, or a snack with someone who needs it. We love you and want to please you! In Jesus' name, amen.

"Share with God's people who are in need"

(adapted from Romans 12:13a).

Peter and John Heal a Lame Man

Acts 3:1-10

What you need:

For each child...
- 1 copy of page 99

You'll also need...
- paper grocery sacks
- Coloring Creations Kit

What to do:

Write children's names on their pages. On each activity page, cut holes (about 1/2-inch in diameter) at the top of the man's legs. Set out crayons, paper grocery sacks, and safety scissors.

1. Give each child an activity page. Explain that the man in the picture couldn't walk; his legs didn't work. Because he couldn't walk, the man couldn't work, and so he had to beg for food or money.

2. Help children cut pieces of grocery sacks that are large enough to cover the man's clothing. After children have cut the paper pieces, allow them to crumple the paper, then uncrumple it and glue the paper to the man to make his rough, worn clothing.

3. Tell children that Peter and John were two men who knew and loved God. They saw the man and said, "In the name of Jesus, get up and walk." And the man got up and walked!

4. Show children how to slip their fingers through the holes in the paper so their fingers become the man's legs. Read children the Scripture verse, and let them wiggle the man's "legs" as they repeat it with you.

Talk about:

Ask: • What "good things" did Peter and John do?

• What good things can you do for people in your home? In your neighborhood?

• How does doing good things show God's love?

Say: God had a special plan for Peter and John...and for the man who couldn't walk. When Peter and John helped the man, he could run and walk and praise God! When *we* help people and do good things, the people we help can praise God, too. God made us to do good things for him. We're like a beautiful picture—a masterpiece—that God made!

Pray: Wonderful God, we are amazed at your power and the great things we can do through you. Show us ways we can do good things for people around us to show them your power and love. We pray that people's hearts and lives will be changed when we do good works for you. In Jesus' name, amen.

"For we are God's masterpiece"

(Ephesians 2:10a).

The Road to Damascus

Acts 9:1-19

What you need:

For each child...

• 1 copy of page 101

You'll also need...

• black markers
• cups of water
• colored chalk
• Coloring Creations Kit

What to do:

Write children's names on their pages. Set out black markers, colored chalk, and cups of water.

1. Give each child an activity page. Tell children that the man in the picture is named Saul. At first, Saul didn't like people who followed Jesus. In fact, Saul wanted to hurt people who followed Jesus. Let children color Saul's robe with a black marker to remember that Saul didn't know or follow Jesus.

2. Explain that one day, Saul was walking to a city called Damascus, when a bright light shone down on him. All of a sudden, Saul couldn't see. Let children dip yellow chalk into water and color the streams of light with the colored chalk.

3. Tell children that Jesus spoke to Saul, telling him to get up and go to a certain place in Damascus. Saul's friends helped him get to the place. While he was there, God told a man named Ananias—who loved God—to go help Saul. When Ananias touched Saul, suddenly Saul could see again.

4. Explain that Saul changed—in fact, he even changed his name to Paul. Paul spent the rest of his life teaching people about Jesus! Let children color Saul's robes (and the rest of the picture) with colored chalk, changing the black robes to bright colors. Read the Scripture verse, and explain that when God created a clean heart in Saul, he changed. Saul wanted to tell everyone how great Jesus is!

Talk about:

Ask: • Why do you think God made Saul blind for a little while?

• How did Saul change after he came into contact with Jesus?

• How do you think knowing Jesus can change *your* life?

Say: God blinded Saul, and it sure got Saul's attention! Saul had time to think good and hard about Jesus, and to realize that Jesus *is* God's Son. God created a clean, new heart in Saul and changed Saul's whole life! God wants each of us to have a clean heart, too, so we can serve God and tell others about Jesus. Let's close our eyes and ask God to give us a pure heart.

Pray: Dear God, only *you* can change lives and hearts. Only *you* can take away our sins and give us a clean, pure heart. Please create a clean heart inside each of us. Help us turn away from doing wrong things and find ways to share your love with people around us. In Jesus' name, amen.

"Create in me a clean heart, O God"

(Psalm 51:10a).

Permission to photocopy this coloring page from *Coloring Creations 2: 52 New Bible Activity Pages* granted for local church use. Copyright © Group Publishing, Inc., 1515 Cascade Ave., Loveland, CO 80538. group.com

Peter Helps Tabitha

Acts 9:36-42

What you need:

For each child...
- 1 copy of page 103

You'll also need...
- cotton swabs
- watercolor paints
- cups of water
- facial tissues
- Coloring Creations Kit

What to do:

Write children's names on their pages. Set out crayons, watercolor paints, cotton swabs, cups of water, facial tissues, and glue sticks.

1. Give each child an activity page. Explain that the woman, named Tabitha, got sick and died. Tabitha was a follower of Jesus. She was good and kind to others. Her friends were sad when she died. They washed her body to prepare it for being buried. Let children "wash" Tabitha's picture by painting it with cotton swabs dipped in paint.

2. Tell children that Tabitha's friends called a man named Peter to come right away. Peter was a follower of Jesus, too. Let children color Peter and the rest of the picture with crayons. (This will allow time for the watercolor paint to dry.)

3. Help children lay a tissue over Tabitha's body, gluing one side of it to the paper. Talk about how Tabitha probably had a blanket on her, since she would soon be buried.

4. Remind children that Peter trusted in God. Read the Scripture verse, and have children repeat it after you. Say that Peter knelt near Tabitha and said, "Tabitha, get up." And Tabitha did! Let children pull back the tissue to show Tabitha sitting up.

Talk about:

Ask: • Tell about a time when you were sick. Who helped you?

• Peter trusted God. Why does God want us to trust him?

• How can this story help you remember to trust God?

Say: I bet it was hard for Tabitha's friends to trust that God would heal her—after all, she had already died. But Peter had special power from God, and he trusted in the Lord. When we trust in the Lord, God won't always heal us or make dead people come back to life. But he *will* give us peace and he *does* promise always to be with us. That's why it's good to say, "I trust in the Lord."

Pray: Lord, we *do* trust you. Sometimes we face hard things, and scary things, and things that confuse us. But we can trust that you are bigger than anything we might face. And we trust that you're always with us. And we trust you to take care of us. We love you and are glad to say that we trust in the Lord. In Jesus' name, amen.

"I trust in God"

(Psalm 56:4b).

Peter Is Set Free

Acts 12:4-17

What you need:

For each child...

• 1 copy of page 105

You'll also need...

• shimmery cloth
• paper reinforcement stickers
• Coloring Creations Kit

What to do:

Write children's names on their pages. Cut a small piece of shimmery cloth for each child. Set out paper reinforcements, markers, glue, and the cloth pieces.

1. Distribute activity pages. Point to the bearded man, and tell children that this is Peter—a follower of Jesus. Explain that Peter was put in jail because he preached about Jesus. The soldiers put heavy chains on Peter's hands.

2. Let children stick paper reinforcement "chains" to the rings on the activity page. Children may color the reinforcements with black markers to make them look more like chains.

3. Tell children that other Christians were praying for Peter. Read the Scripture verse, and explain that prayer is powerful. Say that an angel suddenly appeared in Peter's jail cell. Let children each glue the pieces of shimmery cloth to the angel's robe.

4. Tell children that when the angel appeared, Peter's chains fell off, and he was free to go!

Talk about:

Ask: • How did the people's prayers help Peter?

• When is a time that God answered your prayer?

• What is something you're praying for right now?

Say: God always answers our prayers. Sometimes God says "yes," like in this Bible story. Sometimes God says "no" because he has something better in mind. And sometimes God says, "not yet." But God always listens to our prayers and always answers in the way that's best for us. Let's pray to God right now.

Take prayer requests and pray for specific things children are concerned or happy about.

"Prayer has great power"

(adapted from James 5:16b).

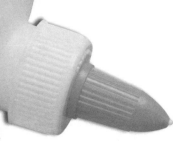

Lydia Believes

Acts 16:11-15

What you need:

For each child…
• 1 copy of page 107

You'll also need…
• plastic wrap
• spray bottle of water
• paper coffee filters
• safety scissors
• Coloring Creations Kit

What to do:

Write children's names on their pages. Set out glue, colored markers, the spray bottle of water, pieces of plastic wrap, and safety scissors. Set the spray bottle to deliver a fine mist.

1. Explain that in the Bible, people made their clothes colorful by dying them with fruit or vegetables. Let children "dye" coffee filters purple by coloring them with markers, then spraying them with a fine mist of water to make the colors run. Set the "cloth" aside to dry.

2. Distribute the activity pages, and point to the man. Let children color the man while you explain that this was Paul, a man who loved Jesus and spent his life telling people about Jesus' love.

3. Explain that Paul came to a river one day, hoping to find a place to pray. Let children color the river blue. Then direct kids to glue pieces of plastic wrap over the blue water to make it sparkle.

4. Tell children that instead of finding a quiet place to pray, Paul found some women sitting near the river. One of the women was Lydia, a woman who dyed and sold purple cloth. Let children cut part of their coffee filter and glue it into Lydia's basket.

5. While children color the rest of the picture, tell how Paul shared the news of Jesus' love with Lydia. Read the Scripture verse, and have kids repeat it. Explain that Paul helped Lydia believe in Jesus. Lydia told her family about Jesus, too. Then they all believed in Jesus, too!

Talk about:

Ask: • Why did Lydia tell her family about Jesus?

• Who is one person you can tell about Jesus this week?

Say: Paul told Lydia about Jesus, and Lydia told her whole family! God wants everyone to believe in Jesus, so it's important that we tell others about Jesus' love and forgiveness. Right now, let's say the names of people we can tell about Jesus.

Pray: Dear God, hear us as we say the names of people we want to tell about Jesus. Let children say the names. Help us to be brave and tell everyone we know about Jesus' love. In his name, amen.

"Believe in the Lord Jesus"

(Acts 16:31a).

Paul and Silas Sing in Jail

Acts 16:16-34

What you need:

For each child...

• 1 copy of page 109
• 5 black chenille wires

You'll also need...

• Coloring Creations Kit

What to do:

Write children's names on their pages. Set out the chenille wires, glue, and crayons.

1. Give each child an activity page and five chenille wires. Let children color the picture while you explain that Paul and Silas were two men who loved and followed Jesus. They were arrested and put in jail for telling people about Jesus.

2. Let children glue chenille wires over the jail bars. Talk about how hard it would be to be in jail, away from your family and friends.

3. Point out that Paul and Silas look happy, even though they were in jail. Explain that Paul and Silas trusted that God would take care of them. In fact, they sang songs to praise God while they were in jail!

4. Have children cup their hands to form a "megaphone." Read the Scripture verse, and have kids repeat it. Then lead children in shouting praises to God through their pretend megaphones.

Talk about:

Ask: • What did Paul and Silas do when they were put in jail? Why?

• When do you like to praise God?

• What's your favorite praise song to sing to God?

Say: Paul and Silas were in a yucky jail cell, but that didn't stop them from praising God. We can praise God all the time! Let's praise God right now.

Pray: Amazing God, you are so worthy of our praise...all the time! Hear us as we shout out our praises to you. Let children take turns shouting praises through their megaphones. In Jesus' name, amen.

"Shout with joy to the Lord"

(Psalm 100:1a).

Scripture Index